Bergerettes = Pastoral ditties : twenty romances and songs of the eighteenth century - Primary Source Edition

Weckerlin, J.-B. (Jean-Baptiste), 1821-1910

Nabu Public Domain Reprints:

You are holding a reproduction of an original work published before 1923 that is in the public domain in the United States of America, and possibly other countries. You may freely copy and distribute this work as no entity (individual or corporate) has a copyright on the body of the work. This book may contain prior copyright references, and library stamps (as most of these works were scanned from library copies). These have been scanned and retained as part of the historical artifact.

This book may have occasional imperfections such as missing or blurred pages, poor pictures, errant marks, etc. that were either part of the original artifact, or were introduced by the scanning process. We believe this work is culturally important, and despite the imperfections, have elected to bring it back into print as part of our continuing commitment to the preservation of printed works worldwide. We appreciate your understanding of the imperfections in the preservation process, and hope you enjoy this valuable book.

M
1730
A42553

CONTENTS

			PAGE
1.	Par un matin	One morning	2
2.	L'amour s'envole	Cupid flies away	4
3.	Menuet d'Exaudet	Exaudet's Minuet	7
4.	O ma tendre musette	Gentle and sweet musette	10
5.	Que ne suis-je la fougère?	Would that I could be the lowly fern	12
6.	Chantons les amours de Jean	Oh, let us sing of the love of John	14
7.	Bergère légère	Capricious shepherd-maid	16
8.	Aminte	Aminta	19
9.	Jeune fillette	Maiden, remember	22
10.	Maman, dites-moi	Mother, please explain	25
11.	Non, je n'irai plus au bois	No, I'll not go to the wood	30
12.	Philis, plus avare que tendre	Phyllis the greedy	34
13.	Non, je ne crois pas	No, I don't believe	38
14.	Trop aimable Sylvie	Sylvia, how I adore you!	40
15.	Venez, agréable printemps	Oh, come again, beautiful Spring	42
16.	Je connais un berger discret	Well I know a shepherd true	44
17.	Nanette	Nanette	46
18.	Chaque chose a son temps	Everything in its time	48
19.	Lisette	Lisette	50
20.	La mère Bontemps	Good old Granny	52

Bergerettes
(Pastoral Ditties)

I
"Par un matin"

I
One Morning

"Par un Matin"

I
Par un matin Lisette se leva,
Et dans le bois seulette s'en alla,
Tra la la la, tra la la dérıdéra

II
Elle cherchait des nids de çà et là,
Dans un buisson le rossignol chanta.
Tra la la la, etc,

III
Tout doucement elle s'en approcha
Savez-vous bien ce qu'elle dénicha?

IV
C'était l'amour, l'amour l'attendait là :
"Le bel oiseau, dit-elle, que voilà!"

V
Son petit cœur aussitôt s'enflamma,
Elle gémit et ne sait ce qu'elle a

VI
Elle s'en va se plaindre à son papa,
En lui parlant, la belle soupira

VII
Il prit l'amour, les ailes lui coupa,
Dans la volière ensuite il l'enferma
Tra la la la, tra la la dérıdéra

One Morning

I
Lisette rose up one morning bright in May,
And to the wood she went alone to play,
Tra la la la, tra la la la lırelay.

II
She looked for birds'-nests all along the way,
A nightingale so sweetly sang its lay.
Tra la la la, etc

III
Lisette walked softly toward the tune so gay,
And found there in his nest—what think you, pray

IV
'Twas Love himself, that sprightly little fay,
"Oh, see the lovely bird!" Lisette did say.

V
Her little heart caught fire without delay,
The strange sensation filled her with dismay.

VI
She went and told her father old and gray,
She was so grieved, her tears she could not stay

VII
He seized that Love and clipped his wings away,
And in the dove-cote shut him up to stay.
Tra la la la, tra la la la lırelay.

II
L'Amour s'envole

II
Cupid Flies Away

"Ô ma tendre musette"

I

Ô ma tendre musette,
  Musette mes amours,
Toi qui chantais Lisette,
  Lisette et les beaux jours,
D'une vaine espérance
  Tu m'avais trop flatté...
Chante son inconstance
  Et ma fidélité.

II

C'est l'amour, c'est sa flamme
  Qui brille dans ses yeux!
Je croyais que son âme
  Brûlait des mêmes feux.
Lisette à son aurore
  Respirait le plaisir;
Hélas! si jeune encore,
  Sait-on déjà trahir?

III

Ô ma tendre musette,
  Console ma douleur;
Parle-moi de Lisette,
  Ce nom fait mon bonheur.
Je la revois plus belle,
  Plus belle tous les jours;
Je me plains toujours d'elle,
  Et je l'aime toujours!

"Gentle and sweet musette"

I

Gentle and sweet musette,
  Breathing my tender lays,
Sing of the fair Lisette,
  And of the by-gone days.
Your notes with love were laden,
  Too much they flattered me;
Sing of the faithless maiden
  And my fidelity.

II

Love with its flame was burning
  Deep in her eyes of fire,
Could not her soul be yearning,
  Filled with the same desire?
Never she dreamed of grieving,
  Never a thought of care;
Oh, that a face deceiving
  Should be so young and fair!

III

Gentle and sweet musette,
  Come and console my pain,
Sing of my lost Lisette,
  Her name brings joy again.
Still I recall with anguish
  Her beauty day by day;
E'en though I grieve and languish
  Love her I will alway.

V

"Que ne suis-je la fougère" "Would that I could be the lowly fern"

Words by Riboutte

Music by Pergolese

suis-je la fou-gè-re, Où, sur la fin d'un beau jour, Se re-
I could be the low-ly fern, Where my love so pure and fair, Seek-ing

po-se ma ber-gè-re, Sous la gar-de de l'a-mour? Que ne
rest at close of day, would turn, Guard-ed safe by Cu-pid's care. Would I

"Que ne suis-je la fougère"

I

Que ne suis-je la fougère,
  Où, sur la fin d'un beau jour,
Se repose ma bergère,
  Sous la garde de l'amour?
Que ne suis-je le zéphyre
  Qui rafraîchit ses appas,
L'air que sa bouche respire,
  La fleur qui naît sous ses pas?

II

Que ne suis-je l'onde pure
  Qui le reçoit dans son sein?
Que ne suis-je la parure
  Qui la couvre après le bain?
Que ne suis-je cette glace,
  Où son minois répété
Offre à nos yeux une grâce
  Qui sourit à la beauté?

III

Que ne puis-je par un songe
  Tenir son coeur enchanté!
Que ne puis-je du mensonge
  Passer à la vérité!
Les dieux qui m'ont donné l'être
  M'ont fait trop ambitieux :
Car enfin je voudrais être
  Tout ce qui plaît à ses yeux!

"Would that I could be the lowly fern

I

Would that I could be the lowly fern
  Where my love so pure and fair
Seeking rest at the close of day would turn,
  Guarded safe by Cupid's care.
Would I were the wind from the south,
  By whose breeze her charms are fed,
Or the air breathed by her tender mouth,
  Or the flower growing 'neath her tread.

II

Would that I could be the placid pool
  Which receives her on its breast,
Or the mantle, clinging, soft and cool,
  Wherein her form is dressed.
I would be her mirror clear and bright,
  Where the beauty of her eyes,
Shining in their own reflected light,
  Fills her soul with glad surprise.

III

Why could I not in her sweetest dreams
  Keep her heart with magic bound,
That the joy which now a vision seems
  Might at length in truth be found?
Yet my hopes are too presuming,
  Tho' inspired by gods above,
For I fain would be assuming
  All the form that charms my love!

VI

"Chantons les amours de Jean"

"Oh, let us sing of the love of John"

VII
"Bergère légère"

VII
"Capricious shepherd-maid"

VII
Aminte
(Tambourin)

VII
Aminta
(Dance-Song)

Poco moderato

Viens dans ce bo-ca-ge, belle A-min-te, Sans con-
Come in-to this grove, my dear A-min-ta, It is

train-te L'on y for-me des vœux. Viens, viens dans ce bo-ca-ge, belle A-
made for the vows of lov-ers true, Come, come in-to this grove, my dear A-

min-te, Il est fait pour les plai-sirs et les jeux.
min-ta, There we'll play, as all hap-py lov-ers do.

Fine

IX
Jeune Fillette / "Maiden, remember"

X

«Maman, dites-moi» "Mother, please explain"

XI

"Non, je n'irai plus au bois" / "No, I'll not go to the wood"

XII
"Philis, plus avare que tendre"

XII
Phyllis the Greedy

Words by Dufresny

Phi-lis, plus a-va-re que ten-dre, Ne ga-gnant
Phyl-lis, of her lov-er a-dor-ing, Greed-y for

rien à re-fu-ser, Un jour ex-i-gea
gain, mi-ser-ly miss, One day in an-swer to

de Syl-van-dre Tren-te mou-tons
his im-plor-ing, Asked thir-ty sheep

XIII

"Non, je ne crois pas" / "No, I don't believe"

XIV
"Trop aimable Sylvie"
(Tambourin)

XIV
"Sylvia, how I adore you!"
(Dance-Song)

Trop ai-ma-ble Syl-vi-e, Plus con-tent d'ê-tre sous ta loi Que si j'é-tais sans toi Roi! Rien ne me fait en-vi-e; Char-

Syl-via, how I a-dore you! Not for a king-dom would I wish my shack-les to un-fet-ter! Naught can tempt me be-fore you; When-

XV
«Venez, agréable printemps» / "Oh, come again, beautiful Spring"

XVI
«Je connais un berger discret»

XVI
"Well I know a shepherd true"

XVII
Nanette

XVII
Nanette

48

XVIII
"Chaque chose a son temps"

XVIII
"Everything in its time"

CPSIA information can be obtained at www.ICGtesting.com
Printed in the USA
BVOW10s1449270514

354582BV00022B/961/P